Original title:
Petals of the Past

Copyright © 2025 Creative Arts Management OÜ
All rights reserved.

Author: Clara Whitfield
ISBN HARDBACK: 978-1-80567-056-8
ISBN PAPERBACK: 978-1-80567-136-7

The Scent of December's Remembrance

In a box the socks do lay,
An old gift from my grandma's day.
She swore they'd keep my feet so warm,
But now they smell like a garlic farm.

With every whiff, I laugh and cringe,
Her love for comfort? A bizarre binge.
Those cozy socks, they tell a tale,
Of laughter, warmth, and a slightly stale.

Wilted Treasures of Memory

A garden filled with gnomes in hats,
Where time forgot to trump the chats.
They nod and chuckle, frozen in glee,
As they witness my failed attempts to be free.

Yesterday's weeds grow wild with pride,
While I declare war, but they won't slide.
I pick a dandelion to make a wish,
And laugh when it's caught by a passing fish.

Fragrant Narratives of What Was

The fridge holds secrets, oh what a smell,
Of leftovers from when we had a swell.
That curry's been living far too long,
It waves hello like an old song.

A bottle of pickle juice in the back,
It sits there waiting for a brave, bold snack.
I sigh and ponder what I might find,
Except a stench that ships me back in time.

A Canvas Painted in Echoes

In closets lurk my childhood wigs,
They still smile, despite the crigs.
Once a princess and then a clown,
Now they laugh at me wearing a frown.

My sketches of cats that looked like ducks,
Each stroke imbued with silly luck.
As I flip through pages, chuckles ring,
Memories dance and joy takes wing.

Shadows of Blooming Dreams

In gardens where the daisies laugh,
I tripped while chasing sunlight's path.
Bumblebees wore tiny hats,
While worms engaged in silly chats.

The sunlit glades are full of cheer,
As squirrels dance, without a fear.
Each flower tells a joke or two,
That make the petals giggle, too.

Withering under the Weight of Time

The roses whisper secrets low,
Of days when they were all aglow.
Now they sigh and droop a bit,
Like grandpas after too much grit.

With every breeze, a chuckle forms,
As aging blooms defy norms.
They reminisce of youthful days,
When bees would buzz in a playful craze.

Petals Unfurled in Distant Days

Once, lilies danced in hats of gold,
With stories fresh and tales bold.
Now they sit with twinkling eyes,
Recalling when they ruled the skies.

The tulips prance with grace and flair,
Sharing moments full of air.
With every gust, their laughter swells,
In whispers only blooms can tell.

The Garden's Memory Lane

Down the lane where blooms once spun,
The daisies played and had their fun.
They'd throw a party, oh what a scene,
Inviting all the flowers green.

Each stem recalls a silly dance,
A waltz of colors, a royal prance.
Tulip tops and petal caps,
Were favorite times with funny snaps.

Fleeting Colors on the Canvas of Days

The crayons of time have all melted,
But the scribbles remain, quite little.
Each hue a giggle wrapped in a smile,
As we paint our tomorrows with silly guile.

Like rainbows that dance when the rain is done,
They twirl in the air, and oh, what fun!
In a world where memories color our strife,
We laugh at the mishaps that flavored our life.

Echoes of Past Youth in the Garden

In a garden where wildflowers chat,
They gossip and giggle, imagine that!
The daisies recall their daring old tales,
Of crushes on bees, and runaway snails.

Swinging on petals, they sing songs of cheer,
As the sunlight dances, twinkling near.
Each bloom a reminder of youth gone awry,
They bloom and they blush, oh how time flies by!

The Wildheart of Long-Lost Blossoms

Once wild and free, like a teasing breeze,
Those flowers have stories that tickle with ease.
They pined for the sun and plotted at night,
Wishing for mischief, oh, what delight!

Their laughter echoes through fateful turns,
Where petals once danced, the wild heart burns.
With each whispered secret from long ago,
They spark funny tales that only they know.

Lingerings of the Springtime Scent

The fragrance of spring is a playful tease,
Like pranks on a breeze that tickle the trees.
It whispers, "Remember that time at the fair?"
Each whiff brings a chuckle, a moment to share.

With cinnamon whirls and a hint of sunrays,
They mingle and come, with their whimsical ways.
As laughter entwines with the sweet, fresh air,
These memories linger, light-hearted and rare.

Spectrum of Time's Wildflowers

In the garden, colors clash,
Old daisies yell, 'We're still in the splash!'
Violets gossip about the trends,
While tulips text, 'Ugly? We'll make amends!'

Sunflowers laugh at flashy buds,
Claiming wisdom from all the floods.
'We bloomed before filters and likes,'
As daisies roll eyes on their bikes.

Withered Stories Under the Stars

Beneath the sky, stories weave,
A clump of daisies, still naive.
They tell of romances with ants,
And where moonlit dreams go for dance.

Their petals curl in disbelief,
Holding secrets like a grumpy chief.
'Last week's wind was quite the prank!'
Now they're just a wobbly plank!

The Aria of Aging Lilies

Lilies hum a tune of flair,
Wisdom gathered in fragrant air.
They claim their beauty's a timeless fib,
While wearing wrinkles like a rib.

'Forget the youth!' they sway and tease,
'Get ready to bloom with a sneeze!'
With laughter sprouting, petals quake,
As bees buzz in for a slice of cake!

Faded Hues of a Bygone Era

Once was red, now slight maroon,
Roses muse, 'Will we be in tune?'
With colors faded, they still boast,
'Our fragrance lingers like a ghost!'

They shake their heads at faux bouquets,
'We lived the thrill of bloom-filled days.'
'No plastic charm or silly spray,
We've danced under the sun's ballet!'

Markings of Nature's Gentle Time

In the garden, weeds have a dance,
Dandelions in a humorous stance.
They giggle as they sprout with pride,
While tulips play coy, trying to hide.

Bees buzzing, they chat and tease,
Waging a war with me, if you please.
Blossoms wink while fending off flies,
Nature's jesters with colorful ties.

Sunflowers stretch and do the twist,
Laughing at shadows that they resist.
Old oak trees, with wisdom profound,
Whisper jokes in a rustling sound.

So let us join in this leafy spree,
Embrace nature's quirks—wild and free.
In hues of green, the world's a jest,
A charming play, who could contest?

Sunkissed Echoes of Past Blooms

A rose that jokes about its age,
Says, 'I'm still fabulous, check my page!'
With petals soft and colors bright,
It giggles at buds, 'You're not my height!'

Laughter lingers in the warm breeze,
As daisies debate who'll win the tease.
Old marigolds reminisce with flair,
'We once stole the show, but who would care?'

Sun-kissed moments slip and slide,
Memories bloom, but none want to hide.
Each flower's tale, a comic delight,
In the grand play of day and night.

Time giggles softly in floral hues,
As we sip sunshine with playful views.
Let's dance through colors, rich and grand,
And scribble our laughter across the land.

Traces of Light on Fading Florals

Faded blooms joke about their wear,
'Could anyone tell? I still have flair!'
With crinkled edges and colors bold,
They share tall tales like a story told.

A violet whispers, 'I'm still a hit!'
While petals drift, a playful bit.
Each shadow holds a chuckle so sweet,
As blooms decline but don't face defeat.

The lilacs snicker, 'Remember when?
We ruled the garden, back then, oh men!'
In this circus of nature's cheer,
Each drooping flower has nothing to fear.

Time's a trickster with a sly wink,
As we laugh and ponder, we begin to think.
In colors soft, we find our song,
In fading hues, we still belong.

Memories in the Fabric of Spring

In spring's embrace, we bloom and jest,
Old tulips claim they're simply the best.
They tour the garden in lavish gowns,
While violets tease with their soft little frowns.

Each breeze brings a chuckle, quite grand,
As blossoms chit-chat while taking a stand.
'You think you're a star?' a daisy will shout,
'Well, I'm the one that everyone's about!'

Bumblebees buzzing bring comic relief,
As they hover around, spreading belief.
'We're the connoisseurs of nectar divine,
But don't tell the moths—they would need a sign!'

So let's laugh with each petal and leaf,
For spring is a tapestry full of chief.
Memories sewn with laughter and cheer,
In nature's quilt, we lose all fear.

Confessions of a Withered Vine

Once I was lush and green,
Now I'm just a funny scene.
Leaves turned crispy, what a shame,
Even the bugs forgot my name.

I tried to dance in the breeze,
But ended up with splinters, please!
Once sang sweet with morning dew,
Now I'm just a side joke, too.

Flowers whispered, "You're too old!"
I nodded, felt the truth take hold.
I laugh a lot for lack of cheer,
Climbing walls with naught but fear.

Oh, to reminisce my vibrant days,
Now I'm humor in a wilted haze.
But here I stand, no need to pine,
With every crack, I make a line.

Tones of an Elsewhere Garden

In a garden where gnomes sway,
They trade stories, night and day.
Roses chuckle, daisies grin,
While weeds just mumble, deep within.

Butterflies wear those silly hats,
Arguing over who's the best at bats.
Crickets chirp a jazzy tune,
While mushrooms giggle under the moon.

The tulips roll their painted eyes,
At laughing daisies in disguise.
Their vibrant colors clash and weave,
Creating chaos none believe.

Every bloom has a tale to tell,
In this hilarity, they dwell.
So if you stroll through vibrant patch,
Brace for laughter and a snappy match.

Stories Sown in the Soil of Memory

Digging deep, what do I find?
Old roots tangled, humor defined.
Potatoes share their tales of woe,
While carrots giggle below the glow.

Once there bloomed a flower bright,
Who daydreamed of taking flight.
But up above, a drone did zoom,
And scared her into a leafy gloom.

Onions weep with laughter loud,
As turnips dance, feeling proud.
Each sprout's a jester in disguise,
Taking jabs with bulging eyes.

So every clod harbors a jest,
Where laughter echoes, life's the best.
With every shovel, joy does bloom,
In this patch, where memories loom.

The Ruins of Floral Reverie

In a world of crumbling grace,
Beauty once wore a glowing face.
Now daisies chuckle at decay,
Turning whispers into a play.

Vines retrace their tangled paths,
While old sunflowers crack up in laughs.
Petals flutter, seeking glory,
But end up stuck in a funny story.

The rose blushes, forgetting pride,
As bees bumble in their joyful stride.
Laughter dances on the breeze,
In ruins where humor never flees.

So we stroll through this quirky plot,
Finding joy in each wobbly knot.
With hearts that giggle in the light,
As memories bloom in playful sight.

Shades of Yesterday's Orchards

In orchards where the apples sway,
Old trees gossip in their own way.
They whisper jokes of squirrels and bees,
And laugh at kids who climb with ease.

The branches dance with fruits so bright,
Wearing shadows in the fading light.
They chuckle at the pies we bake,
While dodging all the worms that wake.

Old trunks wear scars of time gone by,
Experiences written in the sky.
They poke fun at the seasons' mess,
And delight in our youthful stress.

So when you stroll through this old grove,
Listen closely, you might behold,
The laughter wrapped in every leaf,
Reminders that time's not that brief.

Remnants of a Faded Spring

Once the blooms were all ablaze,
Now they hide in their quiet ways.
The daffodils don mismatched socks,
As the tulips trade tales like old clocks.

Bunnies hop with a silly flair,
Chasing clouds through the crisp, cool air.
They giggle at the rain's surprise,
While raindrops dance like tiny pies.

The bees have barbecues 'neath the sky,
Inviting ants but asking why.
They snack on nectar, oh what a treat!
With laughter echoing, oh so sweet!

Faded springs hold memories tight,
With every breeze, an old delight.
They share their secrets in silent swings,
Of days gone by and foolish things.

The Veil of Time's Fragrance

A whiff of yesterday drifts past,
Some scents are sweet, some scents are vast.
The old cologne hangs in the air,
Mixed with laughter and curious flair.

The roses giggle, pink and bright,
While daisies flirt in morning light.
They swap secrets of summer fun,
And reminisce on while they run.

The lilacs sing with voices low,
Confessing tales of love's first glow.
Their fragrance flutters in the breeze,
Carrying echoes of fools with ease.

With every sniff, a tale unfurls,
Of silly pranks and playful swirls.
The veil of scents, a jolly mask,
Hiding smiles in a scented flask.

Blossoms of Longing

With blossoms longing for a cheer,
They try to wave but disappear.
Each petal writes a little tune,
To stir the heart like a bright balloon.

The daisies throw a wild parade,
Where silent wishes are displayed.
They twirl around and lose their hues,
Then trip on laughter, what a ruse!

The violets grumble on their stems,
About their odds against the hems.
They sigh for sunshine, crave the light,
While waiting for a starry night.

Yet in this longing, joy still grows,
In every breeze, the garden knows.
So here's to blooms that grin and sway,
In the sun's embrace, they find their play.

The Blooming Hourglass.

Time tricks us to think we bud,
While old selfies show we've turned to mud.
A flower vase with dust inside,
The moments gone, yet who can hide?

A gardener laughs at weeds that sprout,
They dance like kids at a disco bout.
My memories, like herbs, they stink,
But with a pinch, they help me think.

The seasons change, but who takes note?
An aging rose, a sinking boat.
With every tick, the laughter grows,
Life's just a game, but nobody knows.

So watch your brush and pick your bloom,
Dancing through the inevitable gloom.
In time's embrace, we wear a grin,
For each faded petal, we'll just begin.

Whispers of Forgotten Blooms

Once vibrant colors graced the field,
Now whispers of those blooms, concealed.
In photographs, they pose so spry,
But in reality, they just sigh.

The daisies told the roses bright,
"You'll lose your charm in the moonlight!"
Yet here we are with jokes to share,
As weeds wiggle, unaware, unaware!

Oh, daisies with their frayed edges,
Bursting with tales like fading pledges.
We reminisce on days so light,
While blooms pretend to take their flight.

From sunny days to rainy winks,
Nature laughs while the garden stinks.
Let's toast to blooms so proud and sly,
That catch our hearts but soon say bye.

Echoes in the Garden of Time

In the garden, echoes play tag,
With jokes that wilt, and petals drag.
The marigolds giggle in the breeze,
While daisies plot their sneaky tease.

Forgotten blooms in a silly show,
Each whispering secrets only they know.
The wind carries tales of the past,
Of flowers that bloomed and then fell fast.

With spades and rakes, we dig and pry,
Unearthing laughter, oh my, oh my!
The bees buzz tunes of yesteryear,
And even the compost has its cheer.

So prance through this garden with grin amassed,
As echoes resound, and time flies past.
In blooms of laughter, we find our rhyme,
With every tick of the clock's sly chime.

Dried Fragments of Yesterday

There's a jar full of memories, not so clear,
Dried flowers hiding from last year.
They whisper jokes in a crinkled tone,
"Remember when we felt like foam?"

Each petal shaped like a shattered dream,
But in laughter, they twinkle and gleam.
Oh, some say it's just dust and air,
Yet in the garden, no one can care.

A bouquet of giggles put on ice,
Reminds us that life can be quite nice.
The past is just a silly game,
We laugh so hard, we forget the shame.

So here's to those fragments, stale as they are,
They shine like the funny, fading star.
Each cracked reminder of days gone by,
In the garden of chuckles, we laugh and sigh.

The Secret Life of Fallen Flowers

Once vibrant blooms feel quite ignored,
They reminisce, placing bets on the floor.
A dandelion's giggle, a daffodil's frown,
Together they scheme to take over the town.

In shadows they plan, those ambitious blooms,
Conspiring to paint the grayest of rooms.
With petals like banners, they'll rule the day,
But first, they must rest, 'til the skies go gray.

Reveries in the Overgrown

In the garden of dreams where weeds like to play,
A rogue sunflower claims it will brighten the day.
It dances with daisies, a floppy parade,
While roses roll eyes at the grand masquerade.

The marigolds gossip, taking breaks in the shade,
Whispering tales of each grand escapade.
"Remember that time we took flight on a breeze?"
Now everyone giggles, as dirt bikes tease.

Hallowed Ground of Petal Memories

In a patch of nostalgia, the blooms trade old tales,
Of loves lost and found, and odd, flowery gales.
A lily once swooned for a bee in a tux,
But found his sweet charms came with too many bugs

A tulip once tried to dance with a thorn,
But ended up reeling since the thorn was quite worn.
Through laughter and sighs, they recall all the fuss,
And wonder if love blooms when they're not so plush

A Tidal Wave of Floral Echoes

The petals debate if they're better on ground,
Or flying through air, where the crazy winds abound.
An orchid declares, with a humorous flair,
"I'd rather be art than a poor garden chair!"

But daisies all giggle, their heads in a spin,
Chasing each breeze like a joyful whirlwind.
With whispers and chuckles, they create quite a show,
A cacophony of colors, wherever they go!

A Canvas of Time's Withering Touch

Once I painted all my cares,
With colors bright and wild affairs.
But now those hues have turned to gray,
As I forget where I put my pay.

The brush strokes fade beneath my gaze,
Like those long-lost unfunny days.
I laugh at portraits of my youth,
They sport such joy, but tell no truth.

My canvas now is full of holes,
Where time has pinched my silly goals.
I try to frame my missing sock,
But laughter wins; I must unlock.

So here I stand, with colors bright,
Yet searching for my lost delight.
In every drip, a giggle resides,
For joy is found where laughter hides.

Reminiscence Amongst the Thorns

Amongst the roses, oh what fun,
I dared to dance beneath the sun.
But thorns were sharp, they dug so deep,
I pondered if I should lose sleep.

I twirled and stumbled, oh dear me,
Caught in a bush, awfully free.
Those days of youth, so bright and grand,
Now make me cringe, or shake a hand.

I laugh and wince at each old tale,
Of sticky fingers and grand scale.
I thought I'm brave, a thorny knight,
Turns out I lost — oh what a sight!

Yet still I toast those wild old days,
Where fun once bloomed in silly ways.
Amongst the thorns, a lesson learned,
In laughter's glow, my heart is burned.

The Passageway of Wilted Dreams

In corridors of thoughts I tread,
Past visions that once bloomed, then bled.
Each wilted dream, a funny sight,
With goofy poses, left and right.

I peek around the corners tight,
Where laughter echoes late at night.
A rubber chicken, lifeless, scorned,
Hides in the shadows, barely mourned.

Once, I soared on daring schemes,
Like flying high on sugar dreams.
Now I trip on silly things,
And giggle at what failure brings.

Yet here I walk, through tangled thoughts,
In every fear, a laughter caught.
For even dreams that turn to dust,
Hold humor sweet, if we but trust.

Petals Caught in the Breeze of Memory

Once I ran with blooms in hand,
Chasing laughter across the land.
But here I stand with petals torn,
And just like me, a bit forlorn.

The breeze, it blows, a silly tease,
As memories dance with such great ease.
I chase them down, they flit away,
In every gust, a child at play.

With every splash of color bright,
I stumble over, oh what a sight!
Those days of yore, a smirk appear,
With each remembrance held so dear.

Yet like the flowers, I too sway,
In rhythms sweet, come what may.
For laughter knows no age or stage,
In every bloom, a giggling page.

Echoes of Pollen Memories

In a garden of laughter, bees take flight,
Tripping on petals by morning light.
Old blooms gossip about who made a mess,
While dandelions strut in their floral dress.

A sunflower winks from its sunny throne,
Reminiscing days when it swayed alone.
Forget-me-nots giggle in tiny blue hues,
As daisies declare, "We've got the best views!"

Beneath the roses, there's drama galore,
Thorns whisper secrets they just can't ignore.
With every breeze, a new tale takes flight,
Who knew that petals could bring such delight?

As autumn's breeze takes the blooms on a dance,
A tulip dreams of its springtime romance.
Laughter erupts from the stump of a tree,
"I'm just here for shade, not the gossip spree!"

Chasing the Winds of Remembrance

A breeze flutters past with a cheeky grin,
Carrying tales of where we have been.
The lilacs chime in with their fragrant refrain,
Reminding the violets of their haughty disdain.

Old trees recall when they danced in a line,
While the lazy grasshoppers just sip on their wine.
With every gust, the whispers grow wild,
As petals tumble down like a curious child.

The wind tickles noses, makes everyone sneeze,
While tulips tease pansies with sweet little wheeze.
"Let's race!" cries a daffodil, bright and spry,
As petals go flying, oh my, oh my!

n the chase of those memories, laughter grows thick,
With each twist and turn, it's a classic old trick.
So let's dance with the flowers under skies of blue,
And remember the times that we all thought we knew.

The Fragile History of Blossoms

Once there bloomed a rose quite proud and grand,
   Claiming it knew the best petal brand.
  But whispers from daisies, all soft and sweet,
    Sent its grand tales flying back to its seat.

   Tulips boasted of colors, bold and bright,
    While irises sang in the soft moonlight.
"We're petals of history!" the marigolds cried,
As the wind blew through, giving each bloom a ride.

  A dandelion chuckled, "Let's not take a stance,
   For last week's debate was a floral mischance."
    Yet in every bloom, a giggle resides,
  In the fragile archives of nature's sweet slides.

Chrysanthemums whisper, "Remember that bee?
   It tried to impress with wild poetry!"
  And through this bouquet of miscued delight,
   We dance in the garden till day turns to night.

A Tinge of Eclipsed Colors

In the garden of hues where the zinnias flare,
A lavender blush claiming, "I'm rare!"
But humbles itself with a wink and a sigh,
The marigold beams, "Oh my, oh my!"

Colors collide like a paint splatter fight,
As tulips get tangles in a whimsical plight.
"Let's have a splash party!" chirps a bold fern,
As the daisies rejoice at the chaos we learn.

With hues eclipsed, they're not fading away,
But blooming even brighter in their own unique play.
Cornflowers jest, "We're the real rainbow crew!"
While the violets chuckle, "We'll just tint it blue."

Amidst all the colors, laughter does reign,
As petals of humor dance through the rain.
So let's celebrate blooms, both vibrant and faint,
In this funny old garden where Nature's a saint!

Secrets in the Rustling Leaves

Whispers carried on the breeze,
Tales of squirrels, if you please.
Raccoons plotting grand escapes,
While the trees snap, wearing capes.

Mice gossip about their stash,
Forgotten trails, a fleeting dash.
Jubilant glimpses, secrets shared,
Nature's laughter—who really cared?

Underneath the shady boughs,
Chirping critters raise their vows.
A slapstick dance of leaves and twigs,
While ants perform their circus gigs.

At dusk, the fireflies hit the stage,
With glowing lights, they dance with rage.
They twirl and spin in wild delight,
As shadows laugh in fading light.

Where the Wildflowers Once Danced

In a meadow where dreams do prance,
Old butterflies still try to dance.
With wobbly flaps and silly spins,
Forget the graceful, they're just grins.

Bees buzzing like they own the place,
Sipping sweetness, with a funny face.
Each flower boasts its colorful style,
While daisies giggle a cheeky smile.

A catnap taken by a lazy bee,
Dreaming of honey as sweet as can be.
Poppies chuckle, with heads held high,
As clouds waft low, like a drifting pie.

Here in laughter, the blooms convene,
Chatting of life in pastel green.
With every breeze, their cackles rise,
In this meadow, joy never dies.

Nostalgic Sunlight Between the Petals

Sunbeams dance and play peek-a-boo,
Making shadows, a vibrant crew.
Old memories tickle the air,
With laughter echoing everywhere.

Daisies tell tales of summer rain,
While tulips boast of sunshine's gain.
A playful breeze spins through the day,
Tickling flowers as they sway.

Sun-kissed smiles on every face,
A bumblebee keeps up the pace.
Pollen parties in wild confetti,
Nature's jokes are downright petty.

As twilight falls, the giggles fade,
Flowers rest, their laughter made.
In the hush of night, they'll bloom anew,
Waiting for dawn and the fun to ensue.

Songs of a Forgotten Honeysuckle

Once a band of blooms so bold,
Singing sweetly, tales untold.
Now they hum a rusty tune,
While the moon chuckles at noon.

Vines entwined with playful glee,
Swaying softly, can you see?
Once a party, now a snooze,
The blossoms chat, begin to muse.

A squirrel chimes in, a hushed refrain,
Barking laughter like a train.
Together they croon, with funny flair,
Dancing shadows everywhere.

Old whispers linger in the air,
A tapestry of laughter and flair.
With each breeze, they reminisce,
In their sleepy, vine-wrapped bliss.

A Tapestry of Echoing Colors

In a garden bright with hues,
The daisies gossip, sharing news.
Roses roll their eyes in flair,
While sunflowers pretend to care.

A violette huffs, "I'm the queen!"
While blooms prance with swagger, quite mean.
Petunias sway, in rhythm, get wild,
Stealing the show, like a cheeky child.

Lilies laugh, their scents confound,
A porcupine once roamed around!
Though petals fell with giggles loud,
Nature's jokes will always crowd.

The breeze whispers a silly tune,
As flowers wink beneath the moon.
No grave face among this spree,
Just blooms making history.

The Linger of Old Scents

In corners where the lilacs fade,
People scrub where mischief's laid.
The smell of daisies stuck in time,
From failed bouquets with no sweet rhyme.

An old potpourri of florist's pride,
Where clumsy bees have often tried.
Chrysanthemums snicker, "Have a whiff!"
While geraniums roll on the cliff.

Mirthful thyme skips, "That was my goal!"
As lavender sways, playing a role.
We laugh at scents of bygone days,
In a perfume that still plays.

So here's to those aromas old,
That sing of stories yet untold.
A symphony of odors fine,
With every laugh, a sweet design.

Lost in a Sea of Flowers

Wandering through this floral maze,
Where roses prank and catch your gaze.
Daisies slap me with their cheer,
While tulips giggle near my ear.

"Were you lost?" boasts a peony bold,
"Just follow the sunshine, be consoled!"
With every step, a new bouquet,
An amusing twist to spice the day.

Invisible gnome had left a trail,
In blooms where good jokes prevail.
Pansies tell tales of sneaky bees,
Who once stole hair from breeze-kissed trees.

In this riotous petal sphere,
Lies laughter, love, and not a fear.
So dance through blooms, let troubles cease,
In a garden where joys increase.

Ghosts Among the Petal-Whirls

In haunted gardens where blooms grow,
Ghosts roam with petals soft and slow.
A daffodil shivers, "Who's there?"
A shadow laughs, but who would dare?

The whispers brush against the breeze,
While lilacs float with ghostly ease.
"Boo!" says a marigold, quite spry,
As startled daisies flap and fly.

A squash blossom moans, "I'm feeling blue!"
While phantoms wear their flowery hue.
Robins chuckle from nearby trees,
As blooms giggle at the ghostly tease.

So conspiracy blooms in the air,
A festival of fright, no room for care.
Amidst the colors, joy unfurls,
In gardens where the past swirls.

Whispers of Yesteryear

In a garden of socks, where the gnomes wear hats,
I found my old lunch, with the scent of old chats.
The daisies were laughing, the roses had quirks,
While daisies debated the best way to twerk.

The sunflowers winked with their bright yellow glow,
As bumblebees giggled, putting on quite a show.
The weeds threw a party, and grass danced around,
With critters amused by the sights that they found.

A squirrel stole cupcakes, round and so sweet,
While tulips discussed if they'd ever get feet.
Each whisper I caught, like a tickle on air,
Made me laugh with joy, drowning out all my care.

So here in this chaos, my heart took a dive,
For the winks of the flowers made me feel alive.
In this silly realm, where the past likes to play,
I'll join in the laughter and dance the day away.

Echoes in Bloom

In a field of bright daisies, where shadows take flight,
The lilies are plotting to dance through the night.
With giggles and snickers, the flowers convene,
To share all the jokes that they've heard from the scene.

"Oh, remember that time, when the sun got too hot?
The tulips got sunburned, they couldn't be caught!"
The lilacs erupted with boisterous laughs,
While roses recounted their awkward old gaffes.

The breeze was a jester, tickling each bloom,
As petals spun tales that erased all the gloom.
"I'll challenge the wind to a race across town,
And if I lose, I'll just cover my frown!"

So here in their chatter, the past winks and swirls,
In whispers and giggles, a delight that unfurls.
While echoes of laughter fill up all the air,
I savor these moments, with lightness to share.

Fragments of Forgotten Gardens

In corners once lush, where the flowers were bold,
    The marigolds giggle at stories retold.
With petals like confetti, they sprinkle the ground,
While the snapdragons chatter, and all gather 'round.

"Remember that bee, with a buzz like a train?
He got lost in a blossom and thought it was rain!"
A sunflower chuckled, "Oh, I saw him dive,"
Cracking up with laughter, chasing down a bee hive.

The pumpkins are gossiping under the sun,
And violets tease those who don't join the fun.
Each plant has a tale that tickles the mind,
And as for the weeds, well, they're quite unrefined!

So here in the chaos, with laughter ablaze,
I find joy in the quirks of their whimsical ways.
For in this wild garden, my worries take flight,
As flowers keep laughing, turning day into night.

Memories in Full Blossom

Once in a meadow, where the daisies sway,
A bumblebee buzzed with a game that he'd play.
"Who can outrun me, to the old grassy hill?
I'll take on the flowers; it'll be quite the thrill!"

The tulips were cheering, and the roses, they hollered,
While the pansies just giggled, their petals all collared.
In making the memories, they sparked quite a cheer,
As blooms shared their stories from yesteryear.

"Oh, once I was voted the 'best dressed in bloom,'
But I tripped on a worm—it led to my doom!"
The sunflowers laughed, with their tall, golden heads,
While irises whirled in their party-time threads.

And here in the laughter, the past wears a grin,
As the flowers keep playing, all joining in.
With memories sprouting, and smiles that abound,
These silly old gardens are the best all around.

Tissues of Time's Floral Tapestry

In the garden where daisies dance,
Naps on the petals, not a chance.
A squirrel drops a nut with a loud thud,
Old memories buried right in the mud.

Roses tell stories, but they can't speak,
Secrets and laughter, they all seem cheek.
A bumblebee buzzes, a musician so sweet,
He tries to compose with no rhythm or beat.

Gardening gloves, they tell no lies,
They're stained with tales and a few good fries.
Digging for laughter, we find the dirt,
While weeds crack jokes, we just smirk and flirt.

Sunflowers wink, they're the committee's heads,
Conspiring with daisies, weaving new threads.
As petals fall gently, they land with a pop,
Reminding us all, time won't ever stop.

Whispering Leaves of Old Gardens

The old oak tree spreads its arms wide,
Whispering secrets from the time it tried.
Laughing at squirrels who gather their stash,
And hide them away in a big leafy crash.

Tulips gossip as they sway to the beat,
Of bees in a hurry, not missing a treat.
Over the carrots, the rabbits conspire,
Cackling and munching with greed and desire.

Violets chuckle, a rare shade of blue,
As the roses blush, caught in the view.
Time has a knack for turning things bright,
But leaves just keep laughing, from day into night.

A breeze rustles memories, crisp and fun,
In gardens where laughter will never be done.
With petals so colorful, all in a swirl,
Even the daisies know how to twirl.

The Stain of Time on Beauty's Canvas

An artist once painted a field full of glee,
But spilled some paint while sipping his tea.
The colors got mixed, a whimsical sight,
Now purple and green have a duel every night.

Lily pads float, with a wink and a grin,
They tease the goldfish with their playful spin.
The canvas of time, it smudges and fades,
As the sun throws shade, in sweet serenades.

Old paintings giggle in their frames so tight,
While the brush strokes debate who's wrong and who's right.
A petal fell down, and it landed quite bold,
Now every hue's accompanied by tales often told.

So here's to the stains that make art so grand,
With a whimsical touch from a clumsy hand.
Though the beauty may fade, it evolves and it bends,
Just like the laughter of old, cherished friends.

Unraveled Threads of Floral Histories

In a patchwork of blooms, all tangled and neat,
Lies the tale of a vine where the flowers retreat.
Grandmother's laughter, like silk on a spool,
Gets tangled with whispers, it's a magical fool.

Faded old memories unravel with cheer,
While daisies draw near, their stories so dear.
They twirl and they twist, like ribbons of time,
Frolicking joy in a rhythm so prime.

Roses remember the crush of a bee,
Who once wore a crown, so bold and carefree.
Each petal a token, a fragment so bright,
Of stories and giggles that dance in the light.

As threads intertwine, with folly and flair,
The floral parade takes us everywhere.
In laughter, in color, with whimsy we sing,
The grand tapestry blooms, as the seasons bring.

Castles in the Air of Nostalgia

Once I built a tower tall,
Where dreams would dance and shadows sprawl.
But legos broke and plans fell through,
Now I sip tea, just feeling blue.

I once envisioned grand delights,
With space robots and satellite flights.
But pets knocked down my DIY plans,
Now they rule as furry fans.

I played the king, I played the knight,
Yet found my throne was half a sight.
My paper crown, a grand display,
Flew out the window, oh what a day!

So here's to castles made of air,
With moments lost in laughter's flare.
Though bricks are soft and dreams may fall,
With silly thoughts, I have it all.

The Aroma of Wistful Shadows

The scent of cookies fills the hall,
A memory of baking's call.
I mixed the flour, forgot the eggs,
Now I just hug my blurry legs.

With gingerbread men all askew,
Their icing faces feel so blue.
I set a trap for Santa's crew,
But ended up stuck in a shoe!

The shadows dance, they laugh and tease,
Remembering spilt juice and bee stings.
I wave at ghosts of times gone by,
While munching snacks, with crumbs awry.

Yet still I find a chuckle bright,
In every splatter of my plight.
The aroma lingers, sweet and fat,
As laughter echoes where I sat.

Hushed Conversations with the Blooms

The daisies whisper in the breeze,
'You picked the wrong plant, oh what a tease!'
I gaze at blossoms, big and small,
Thinking how my talents fall.

In the garden, mishaps bloom,
A cactus next to sweet perfume.
I watered weeds and chattered loud,
While bees concocted their own crowd.

Roses laughed with petals spread,
'You should have learned this, go back to bed!'
I waved to violets in disdain,
As they rolled their eyes, oh what a pain!

So I retreat, a gardener shy,
With dreams of flowers soaring high.
Still every bloom brings me delight,
In chats with petals, oh what a sight!

Fragrant Reminiscences

I once found treasures in the dirt,
When digging deep, I found a shirt.
Buried socks and half a shoe,
A treasure chest, oh who knew?

The scents of summer fill the air,
But now it's fedora wear and hair.
Old memories cling like sticky goo,
I laugh at selfies that I drew.

With each whiff of the blooming time,
I recall the hills, the sloshing slime.
Those joyous days, a fragrant mess,
With every memory, I confess.

So raise a toast to those old days,
Where laughter lingered, warmth plays.
For fragrant joys and silly dreams,
Are life's bouquet, or so it seems!

Diary of a Faded Bloom

I found an old flower, all crumpled and torn,
Its scent claimed it fresh, but it's clearly worn.
It tried to impress with its wilting charm,
But even a bee just rolled its arm.

A snail popped by, said, "What's that smell?"
He thought it a prank, like some bad spell.
With whispers of fragrance, it feigned delight,
But blooms with more color just laughed at its plight.

The petunia gossiped, its gossip was grand,
About how the lily had trouble to stand.
In this garden of stories, all wilted and frail,
The echoes of laughter still tell us the tale.

Yet under the sun, with a chuckle or cheer,
Even the faded can shine, have no fear.
For laughter's a flower that never will die,
And who knows, tomorrow a new bloom may try!

Silhouettes of Time on Fragrant Wings

In the garden of yesterdays, shadows flit by,
With butterflies giggling, as time wanders high.
A daisy exclaimed, with a laugh and a sway,
"Hey, who brought the weeds to our flowery play?"

The roses just snickered, as thorns poked about,
While daisies debated what life's all about.
"Do we dance in the breeze, or just sway in the sun?"
A bee buzzed in, said, "Let's make this fun!"

Memory's a butterfly, flapping its wings,
In bright, foolish colors, it jovially sings.
"Oh look at my past, in a funny old hue!"
Laughter danced on petals, in shades bright and blue.

So come join the laughter, where blooms intertwine,
With stories of joy in the garden divine.
For every wedding of blooms, with quirks in the air,
The scents of nostalgia are a fragrant affair!

Whispers of the Flowering Shadows

The shadows chattered softly, like whispers at dawn,
As daffodils teased the old lilac's yawn.
"Have you noticed that we're dating the lore?"
The lilac just chuckled, "At least I'm not snore!"

Each blossom a gossip, with stories to share,
About how the daisies went wild with flair.
They threw quite the party, with pollen as wine,
But the clumsy old daffodils tripped on the vine.

With petals like confetti, they danced round and round,
While tulips coordinated a prank on the ground.
"Let's swap all our colors!" they giggled in glee,
A rainbow of chaos that tickled the bee!

Yet in all this jesting, the shadows will gleam,
For laughter is sunlight, a glorious beam.
In laughter's embrace, we find spirits that soar,
While whispers of flowers enchant evermore!

Chronicles in Nature's Quietude

In a nook of the garden, where silence prevails,
A weed wrote a book with impossible tales.
"I was once a fine rose, but then came the hoe!
Now I'm just here with my friends, on the low."

Lilies turned to daisies and chuckled a bit,
As the fern told a story of being a twit.
"I chased off a bug, but it turned out too wise,
And now I'm just here looking up at the skies."

The trees stood around, rolling rings in their bark,
Listening to banter from dawn until dark.
"What's youth without laughter?" the petals thus sighed,
As the tales of the garden continued to bide.

Each leaf a reminder of laughter and cheer,
In this quiet abode, where hearts draw near.
For every sweet memory and chuckle we clutch,
Nature whispers back, in a soft, loving touch!

Remnants of a Floral Dream

Once a rose danced in a breeze,
Now it's stuck in a sneeze.
Laughter echoes through the air,
As petals tumble without a care.

A daffodil played hide and seek,
Worn out shoes, oh what a peak!
In a pot, a memory glares,
Of botanical love that just wasn't there.

Daisies giggle, their heads held high,
Whispering secrets to the shy.
With every glance, stories unfold,
Of dreams once green, now rusted gold.

Sunflowers reminiscing their youth,
Mixing truth with a dash of goof.
For every faded bloom's delight,
There's laughter tucked in leafy night.

Time's Tattered Bouquet

A bunch of stems with stories to tell,
Some made us giggle, some not so well.
Once vibrant hues have dulled with age,
Each blossom still plays a funny stage.

Lilies laugh as they start to wilt,
They're dressed in a cloak of forgotten guilt.
Meanwhile, tulips strike a pose,
In odd-shaped vases, they strike a prose.

Chrysanthemums in a spotlight flash,
Telling tales of a flowered bash.
With each wilted petal and flickering smile,
Time makes sure we can laugh for a while.

So when you stumble on old floral scraps,
Remember the giggles and the happy mishaps.
What once was a garden, now a playful jest,
In our hearts, they continue their quest.

The Scent of Lost Seasons

In the air wafts a funky smell,
Of blossoms that once rang the bell.
A cheerful tune, a floral dance,
Now forgotten in a dusty trance.

Crisp autumn leaves make a hat,
For a sunflower that once was fat.
They play dress-up, a show so bright,
Fading memories, but still polite.

Smells of lavender, with a twist of cheese,
Bringing smiles, a floral tease.
As daisies reminisce about June,
And waltz with shadows to a silly tune.

When seasons shift and blooms take flight,
Giggling softly in the fading light.
Each flourish reminds us to find the grin,
In every wilt, there's a story within.

Blooms Beneath the Dust

Underneath the soil, whispers rise,
Of flowers that told the best lies.
But now they're trapped in a dusty affair,
As weeds tell jokes, unaware of their wear.

The violets chuckle in silence deep,
About how the gardener forgot to weep.
Roses roll on the floor in mirth,
Joking 'bout their royal birth.

A posy of pansies, with humor so bright,
Study the clouds, oh what a sight!
As petals fall with a joyful shout,
They whisper secrets, giggling about.

And in this garden of wayward dreams,
Laughter echoes with hidden schemes.
For life's too short for gloomy fuss,
Let's raise a cheer for blooms and dust!

If Flowers Could Remember

If daisies told tales, oh what a fuss,
They'd gossip 'bout bees in a clumsy bus.
Roses would laugh, so proud and so spry,
While tulips will blush, and wonder why.

Sunflowers snicker, each facing the sun,
"I'm taller than you!" oh isn't it fun?
Violets would mumble, shyly retreating,
While the lilies hum soft, the rhythm pulsating.

A daffodil's dance, with a twist and a twirl,
"I'm the brightest!" it claims, amidst leaves in a whirl.
And daisies would roll, on the soft grassy floor,
As the wind tells a joke, and they all roar.

What mischief they'd weave under skies so blue,
These blossoms would surely outsmart me and you!
But the memories fade in a gust of delight,
And they'd giggle until the fall of the night.

Shadows of Time Amongst the Stems

In the garden of whispers where shadows pose,
The herbs tell secrets, like leaves in a prose.
"Remember that time when we grew in a line?"
"Oh yes! I was wild, and my neighbor was fine!"

Butterflies chuckle, with gossipy flair,
As petals recall pranks from a mischievous air.
"You thought you were grand, swaying in style!"
"But I danced like nobody, just for a while!"

The fragrance of laughter, it lingers so sweet,
As sunlight sneaks through, shakes off its defeat.
However, the dust bunnies beneath the rose bed,
Will just laugh and roll over, filling hearts with dread.

But in this wild garden, where laughter bears fruit,
A day of old tales sprouted in root.
So here's to the stories that bloom like a smile,
With shadows of time growing richer in style.

Moments in a Blooming Silence

In the hush of the garden, when sunset begins,
The flowers exchange their confounding spins.
"Did you see that bee, tripping over the fern?"
"He flew like an acrobat! What a twisty turn!"

A whispering breeze pulls a petal from place,
And the daisies make jokes about their lost grace.
"He lost his balance, poor thing, what a plight!"
As tulips chime in, giggling into the night.

Hydrangeas huddle, snug under the sky,
Then burst into laughter, oh my, oh my!
"What's next for us blooms? A race to the fence?"
"Or a contest for pollen? Let's create some suspense!"

Thus moments go by, in delightful excess,
With chuckles and grins, they could not care less.
These blossoms in silence, so joyful—so spry,
Create joy in their stillness, as day passes by.

The Elegy of Seasonal Changes

As summer does bow graciously to fall,
The blooms five o'clock are not ready to stall.
"Why choose between frost or a sun-kissed affair?"
Said marigolds while preening their hair.

In a twilight that flickers with whispers and cheer,
The autumn leaves giggle, caused by all they hear.
"Remember those jokes of last spring's coy rain?"
While preparations for winter bring chuckles again.

"Oh what will you wear?" the ferns curiously tease,
As asters wear layers, all rustling with ease.
"You'll freeze, my friend, look at your silly shoes!"
Leaves tumble and roll, unleashing their views.

Hues shift and tumble, oh nature's grand jest,
As blooms pull their coats, snuggly to rest.
Yet amidst all the changes, in laughter they bind,
The beauty of seasons, so whimsically kind.

www.ingramcontent.com/pod-product-compliance
Lightning Source LLC
Chambersburg PA
CBHW071815160426
43209CB00003B/101

9781805670568